SUSAN EH THOMAS
ADULT COLORING HUE KNEW? Series

USING THE POWER AND PSYCHOLOGY OF COLOR TO HEAL & DESTRESS

"Gratitude"

WWW.YOURADVOKIT.COM

Published by YourAdvoKit Publishing
Maryland, USA
Email: susan@youradvokit.com
www.YourAdvoKit.com

Copyright © 2017 by Susan EH Thomas
All rights reserved. No part of this publication
may be reproduced, stored in a retrieval system, or transmitted, in any or any means, electronic,
mechanical, photocopying, recording or otherwise, without prior permission from the author.

A whopping 74% of the population is stressed out. And most all of us want to find relief but don't know how. Or know how, but are too embarrassed, or don't have the time, or worst-case scenario, we don't have the emotional energy to put forth the effort. It's a double edge sword, a dangerous cycle, a dead end.

What - Do - You - Do?

You take baby steps, you take one small bite at a time. And with each bite digested, every ounce of courage gained...you grab another piece of freedom, faith, accomplishment and then you take another bite.

Listen, this coloring book isn't going to radically change your life, or even solve your worst problems...but it is a really good tool to have in your mental health toolbox. And you can never have too many of those.

What separates the "Hue Knew?" series from most other adult coloring books?

Each coloring book comes with a suggested color scheme. These are the colors chosen that work best with the topic of the book [Gratitude, Exciting Opportunities, Positive Thinking.] All colors have certain meanings **and** they all spark or avert certain emotions. I've applied the science behind the color [aka color psychology] and incorporated it into the drawing on the page; giving you the fullest, positive emotional effect.

Of course, you're not held prisoner to these color choices. And can color them whatever hue makes you most happy. After all, isn't that the [colored pencil] point? At the end of the day, for most people who are drawn to coloring books – are seeking a resemblance of peace and a sliver of joy.

Directions: It's okay to go outside the recommended color scheme. But using the colors suggested predominately and **variations of** throughout your coloring sheet best triggers the emotions they're associated with.

BTW: Other than the psychology of color, there's not a lot of difference between me and all the other wonderful coloring books sold online and off, today. I've never viewed myself, or these books as a "competition" because at the end of the day the coloring book for adults is extremely therapeutic.

I'm honored to stand amongst all Adult Coloring Book Authors and encourage you to partake in a variety of these books - as we all have a little something different and unique to offer. And you shouldn't put all your eggs in one basket – or rather, in this case – colored pencils to just one brand of coloring pages!

Color Swatch for "Gratitude"

Green | Orange | Yellow

[To view the swatch in color online go to YourAdvoKit.com/HKG.html]

The subject of gratitude can be a touchy one. Because even the most compassionate, giving person may fall into the "ungrateful" trap. It's not that they're bad people – it's that they're human, and no one is perfect, and sometimes being selfish is about survival or for our own good. That being said:

When you're grateful, it clears the path for where you want to be and the things you wish to conquer. The more often you show your gratitude, the more good things you'll receive in return to be thankful for. When you're grateful, you're better able to realize even the challenges in your life, happen for a reason. And as luck would have it...you're grateful for the lessons you learn from those very challenges!

The colors orange, yellow and green all emote emotions or evoke feelings, that encourage graciousness. I often suggest using these coloring sheets when you know you're facing a situation in which you'll need an extra boost of "gratitude" or whatever is the subject of the book.

Strive to feel grateful every day. Not just when coloring, and using the colors orange, yellow and green...but make a conscious effort daily to thank your children for a job well done – thank your friends for being there – thank your mate for listening – thank your co-workers for being helpful – and thank God, your lucky stars or whomever your higher power may be, for another great day!

> Remember; you're not married to using only these colors. You can use variations of and/or move outside of this color palette all together. But to get the fullest "Hue Knew?" effect, try and use the colors suggested [and variations of] predominately. If you're coloring the pages for pure pleasure...then throw the color scheme out the proverbial window and color your world whatever hue makes you happiest!

Many of these pages are "frames" or are created with space for you to write your favorite quotes or affirmations or even doodle your own artwork inside of them.

Enjoy!

About the Author

I was born, and raised in the beautiful Appalachian Mountains on the East Coast in Maryland. And have 2 teenage sons...Jake and Luke. It is because of them I work so hard, and dedicate so much time – in the area of emotional health. I think most of us who have children become more aware of our surroundings after they're born. Most specifically the environment and global warming. We try and do better to take care of it as best as we can. For me, it's mental health [although I recycle too:] as it negatively affects both sides of our family, and deeply. But it's a worldwide problem too. I'm well versed in this area and on many levels - so for the past 15 years, I've dedicated my life to contributing to mental awareness, self-help, suicide prevention, healing and the methods of. Not just for me & my family...but for all in need of emotional stability. I'm certified in Color Theory - and in what I call a perfect storm, I'd combined my education with my life experiences and began "YourAdvoKit." A community for all those in need of a friend and support. And I will spend the rest of my life supporting and helping those in need of emotional support. It's my passion; and it's been an honor. Because it takes a village, and if you'll allow me to be a part of yours...I'm in! – Hugs, Susan

The Buck Doesn't Stop Here!

Download FREE and fun resources, life hacks, printables, quotes and guides that help improve your quality of life & promote a healthy mind - all while living your life less stressed at **YourAdvoKit.com**

Bundles for Enhancing Your Mental Health Including:

- The Law of Attraction for Easing Depression
- The Emotional Freedom Technique [EFT] or Tapping
- Meditation for Easing Depression
- Mindfulness and Mental Health

Life Hack/Tip Sheets Including:

Procrastination | Never Give Up | Be More Open Mind | Simplify Your Life | Spirituality | Be More Outgoing | Motivation | Become More Giving | Embrace Discipline | Exude Confidence

Getting the Girl: Compassionate, real life, relationship advice. "Getting the Girl" is a beautifully written publication while maintaining an honest balance of respect and truth. While written for men, the advice can be applied to all...as manners, respect, kindness and love have no boundaries and should be shared and given in abundance no matter the technicalities.

Goal Setting Information and Downloadable Infographic

Coloring Books

More "Hue Knew?" Coloring Books

Not everyone uses coloring books to ease depression, soothe anxiety or boost self-esteem. But for those who do, and because with all my heart I want to make a difference, even if it is just a small contribution...I've also a set of affirmation cards that compliment this coloring book and its theme for download and they are yours FREE! They are beautifully done in the same color scheme as this coloring book and are the size of a business card for your convenience; to be laminated, cut and carried with you and read daily until the affirmation truly resonates.

They're on the same page as the color swatch I mentioned at the beginning of this book. Enjoy!